The Sista Girl's *Manifesto*

ISBN (978-0-578-84079-6)

Printed in USA

Dedication

I would like to dedicate this book to my living Grandmother Juanita Moore and my late Grandmother Emma Ingram, and all the elder women in my family. I especially dedicate this collection of poems to the young women that are coming up behind me. May this book bring healing, education, and reflection as you transition from Girl to Woman.

Table of Contents

Foreword

A scripture in the Bible says, "A Man's gift will make room for him, and bring him before great men." Well in this case, we have an amazing woman who is not just gifted, but amazing and full of grace and ambition. What makes her gift so amazing? It's something she has paid for with her life and many hard times. Yet, she is willing to share it with those who may not know the value of their gifts.

For years, her gift remained a hidden treasure. I believe God wasn't finished wrapping it and he was putting the final touches on her. I believe, now, is the time to unwrap what's been hidden inside of her for so long. I have learned and watched over the years by mentoring, listening, and pushing her, that there was something great locked inside of her that needed nurturing.

I have watched this phenomenal woman bounce back from being broken into pieces to walking in peace. She has had many challenges, and never once did she stop going, although it was not always easy. Many judged her, but through her poetry she speaks truth.

Rose sincerely pours her heart, pain, and healing into her poetry. I have watched her fight her inner pain and struggles by writing them on paper. In the Bible, the book of Habakkuk 2:2 (KJV), says, "And the Lord answered me, and said, Write the vision and make it plain upon tables, that he may run that readeth it." I believe this scripture is speaking to Rose for such a time and season as this. The Sista Girl's Manifesto is a collection of poems that can reach the heart of anyone, because it's different than just reading novels. Many people need to read a story that could speak to them in a series-like kind of way.

S. Rose as she is so affectionately known, is a dynamic writer and example of what she writes. Her ability, to take her life experiences and write them on paper as a guide of freedom for herself and others, is fantastic. This woman will change many lives and cause many to be healed through her poetry. Now, let me say, this book of poetry is not for the immature, but the matured. Not every story is lovely. I am honored first to be her pastor and a reader of her material. I thank God for what he has done in her life thus far. There is more to come after this.

S. Rose, I leave you and all your readers with this, Romans 8:28. (KJV) "And we know that all things work together for good to them that love God, to them who are called according to his purpose." It all works for you. Just do it!

Sincerely,

Pastor Arvetta L. Woody

Senior Pastor, Evangelism On The Move Outreach Ministry

Preface

The Sista Girl's Manifesto is a collection of poems and conversations for any young girl, young woman, and fully grown woman, who can relate to the struggles of the transition from girl to woman. This book was designed to not only shine the light on the trials and tribulations of the growing pains that a young woman experiences, but the triumph of her pain. Go with me, as I unpack many layers of my mistakes, due to Low Self- Esteem, Low Self- Worth, Lack of Self- Respect, and Self- Love. On this journey of womanhood, we learn what it takes to fully and honestly, love the skin we are in. While one can receive love from another source, I am learning that love can only be fulfilling when it comes from within. Take a ride with me, as I trip and fall and bust my lip a couple of times, as I am going

Chapter One

Conversations with Granny

Be the best. I'm grateful to have a grandmother that's alive and well. I was blessed to have both of my grandmothers till I became an adult. My father's mother passed away from Cancer when I was a few days shy of my 21st Birthday; Emma Ingram was her name. I had great regret for not spending enough time with Grandma Emma in my teen years. We were tight until she hurt me by a small misunderstanding. May she continue to sleep in Peace. I wish that we could've talked about it. I was too immature to think that way then. I lost years because of my stubbornness. However, I couldn't make up the time with her, but I make sure I do right by Grandma Nina. One thing that I learned from my grandma Emma is not to take people or unique relationships for granted. Even in death, she was still teaching me how to love, forgive, and let go of the past so I can have a fruitful future. There's restoration in forgiveness. My mother's mother is named Juanita; I'm her namesake. My mother honored her by giving me her first name as my middle name. As of this date, I make sure I do not hold grudges with her about anything; I check on her often, see her and spend time with her. She loves when I come over. We sit and talk about her life growing up with my great grandma Minnie. I now understand why Grandma Nina takes no shorts. Her mother Minnie didn't either; I guess you can say I come from women with fire in their bellies. We would call them strong, black women, who aren't afraid to be soft, kind, loving and ladylike. Granny and I have a lot in common. She was once soft- spoken and would be easy going with people, until she learned that people would run a marathon over you if you let them.

She advised me to be nice, as that is my nature, but don't take any mess from anybody. Sometimes, I fall back into my old ways of being passive. Although she is alive, I can still hear her voice telling me, "don't let anyone talk to you in any kind of way." She learned that by getting sick and tired of abuse from her first husband and even her mom at times. She grew up independent. She had to learn how to cook at an early age, while her mother worked. I guess one can say she learned survival early in life. I love how resilient my granny is. She may not know many fancy words or even know how to do calculus, but she knows life, and I respect her. Now, my Granny isn't your typical get some ice cream type of granny. Yes, she will feed you; However, she will also lay into your behind if you're going in the wrong direction. She has no filter. Sometimes, she says things that can be perceived as quite rude; some may call it sharp. She speaks her mind though, and you know where she's coming from at the end of it all. You will know she's not trying to hurt you. She's just being honest about it. People speak of generational curses often, but how about generational blessings, generational love, generational wisdom. I've been fortunate enough to experience all of them by having a mother who consistently prays for me and has also taught me how to pray for myself. My grandmother, who shares her wisdom with me through conversations, teaches me how to manage the mistakes I have made in my life but helps me to understand life's lessons. I am blessed. I now appreciate my complexity after learning the strength of the women that came before me. I understand more and more the value of being a strong, black woman. It doesn't consist of neck twisting, finger- snapping, or telling a person off about themselves that makes me tough. It is in my ability to be soft, turn away wrath, use wisdom, and be beautiful and ladylike, all while being a courageous woman. I am broken, but resilient, I am weak, but strong. I am a sinner saved by grace. I do not know it all, but I'm willing to learn. I am not my mistakes; However, I have made some. I am the women that came before me. I now understand why granny used to say...

Granny use To Say,

"A Hard Head Makes A Soft Behind."

Sis

Thinks

She's

Grown

Don't Get Burnt Out Before You Get Fully Lit

Don't get burnt out before you get fully lit. Switching them hips and dragging that wagon. If you are not careful, you will be burnt out before you get fully lit. These boys are known for waxing that sass right off the ass of many. Leave you wiping your pretty, little tears with an old Basketball Jersey. Wait your turn, do not get burnt out before you can get fully lit. You have time to click those heels down avenues and streets, meeting your homegirls and talking of sizes of their meats. He whispers sweet nothings in your ear, making you smile, it might turn into tears, if you are not careful. Maybe even spoil you. Rotten you to your core. Be careful! Stay sweet, be gentle. Princes can be charming, so do not get burnt out before you get fully lit.

Sour Peach

*House cat never knew street shit, but still
had to beat shit. Addiction had me in heat,
the devil got me moving my feet. Every
blue moon, call me smokey to escape
defeat, but still had to deal with losses.
Negative thinking had me creating losses.
Too broke to floss, but no guts to steal
from stores. Bump laws, never cared
about rules, my God, so many rules.
School kept me grounded, I mean, granny
kept me grounded. Lessons in life keep me
from being trife. I Used to care about
being right, getting my point across,
would even fight. Verbal spats and nasty
sex on the constant. We make up to break
up. Sis got tired of picking my face up.
Ok, heard 'em say, Change Gon come.
Hopefully, tired of counting change, I'm
numb. Still young, dumb, and full of cum.
Verbal beatings, soon to overcome.*

Wake Up

Wish I could be deep as oceans and write lyrics that will make 'em want to do more than cum, but I'm still numb from my twenties and all the poor decisions that help diminish me. I mean, it didn't demolish me, but it dismantled me. Somebody pass me some gorilla glue. Wish I could be as deep as the oceans, but my thoughts are so limited. From time to time, thought life gets crippled between how I thought he would be a quick fix and miraculous. Make me whole with the throb of his penis, and a gentle but firm squeeze on my left butt cheek. Maybe he can teach me some self -respect, but instead, he teaches me perfect lies. He impregnates me; then I start believing the lies are the truth. Oh, this shit gets deep. Not to mention. I got to pay this rent, but on the other hand I'm still trying to look fly. You know, still thinking of things with no substance, but I just chalk it up as human nature, but in all reality, it's just vain, dumb shit. Every now again, I might tune in to a news station or breeze through the eyewitness news app, not important enough to pick up a paper, which proves what racist whites say about blacks. It is the same things going on, racism, political bullying, Klan members in blue uniforms claiming to protect and serve but they're only serving pistols with heat from gunpowder that shatters vessels destroying yet another one of God's vessels that he put here. We have parents abusing and killing their children. The same ones that yell they don't believe in abortions, but you tell me, what's the motherfuckin difference? Some of us are still lost. I'm no better, I just respond with, damn, this shit is crazy, and press the button on the bottom of my iPhone to close the application that I couldn't even afford, but still bought, just to have it. That just sounds wack. The truth of the matter is I don't even use all the functions that Apple says there are. Not to mention, I am still functioning with broken pieces. Never mind who did it because it's my responsibility to fix it; perhaps then I could get past being governed by my emotions and live a life outside of the four chambers of my brain, maybe then I could finally leave the radius of my long narrow block.

Shit, I'm sometimes stuck between consciousness & unconsciousness. Am I a black woman full of purpose? Or am I nothing but a childish nigger thot? Harsh, but I'm just trying to figure out my shit.

Wish I could be as deep as the oceans and write lyrics that will make 'em want to do more than cum, but I'm still numb from my twenties and my thoughts are sometimes so limited. Perhaps I should spend less time on the gram and do some research and find out who I really am.

Fed Up

The festering, the arguing, wishing I was dead instead of living. Just breathing, trying to make a living. Funds aren't right, in my mind constant fight. Bipolar every other night. I'm taking flight. Got to be more to life than chasing niggas, getting tight.   Laying on my back to make shit right. Nah, I'm fed up. This pussy ain't trash. Niggas treating me like trash then heading for the dash? On my new shit. Fuck that dick. Getting my money right. Shit got to give because my mind stays in a fight. Who's going to win? Me or you? I tell you I'm through. Low Self Esteem, fantasies, and dreams? Now I'm on my real shit, ready to deal shit, can't run from the pain. Nigga this is me, I'm here shit.

This Thing Called Drama

*I get nurtured from it. Sort of kind of like
how a baby sucks the milk out of a
chocolate Areola from it, an instinct to it,
straight from the womb to it. I don't want
anything but it. I live for this shit. It fuels
me, and my subconscious, won't let
anything subdue it. I'm true to this.
Without drama, I'm anxious. I know it's
more to life than it, but I live for this. I'm
scared without it, bored, confused,
nervous. Is there a ground beneath me
without it? It keeps my feet planted. No
please don't take it from me. Don't take it.
Like a child with its favorite Teddy Bear.
Can you guarantee me a life without fear?
I'm fearless with it. At least I feel like I am.
If you promise me, I can still breathe when
drama leaves. I just don't see it. I can't see
it. I mean, it's all I mothafuckin' know.
How could you try and take this from me?
Why would you? It's all I have left to hold*

on to. It's my bread to my butter. It's my peanut butter to my jelly. It's my gold seal on my diploma. That says I made it, I survived it and I can always survive it. So please don't take my drama away. See, I'm a thrill chaser. The thrill of overcoming. It lets me know that I'm strong. What real strength without overcoming? How can I be validated with valor with no battle? How can I say I survived with no scars?

Who gives a fuck if I caused my pain? Well, maybe I do. But who will know? Who will know that I ache like a fiend for its fix when I have peace? Can you hear my cry? Can you hear my voice? It's subtle, but I can hear it. Don't leave me quiet. Quiet scares me. Quiet confuses me. Peace allows me to think. I don't want to think. So please, allow drama to fuel me, and I'll allow peace to fuel you.

Good & Crazy

*See, I have been good & crazy, asked
myself questions and answered them too,
made up stories in my mind, words filled
with grime, deceit, I've sold myself. Down
pits of grief, Good & crazy, I would love to
blame my growing parents, you know,
those that raised me, but some learned
behavior while others were self-taught.
Spoken out of my mouth. I have beaten
down doors that were locked just because I
saw myself in there. Not that God
promised it. There, could have meant
anywhere. I did not care once my mind
was made up. I would drag myself down
hallways, street pits, dig myself a ditch,
and jump in it, then reach up and throw
dirt on myself. Pity parties, I have sworn
that I would conquer and slay Goliath, but
I loved the way he tormented me.*

*I mean I loved the way I tormented me,
call me a cutter, because I have given
myself laceration after laceration, playing
stories over and over in my mind that may
have happened or maybe not even yet. So,
I told myself. Come go with me to a place I
call good & crazy. They call it a
generational highway because this thing
runs deep, deep in my veins, my
subconscious believes things my conscious
has no recognition of. My therapist said, I
must unlearn some things. My pastor said,
I must slay my flesh to change some
things. Are you ready? I said am I ready?
Those lies had me tangled up like a
grapevine. A crown of thorns on my head,
but I am no Jesus. Good & crazy. When
those emotions get heightened, I am a
wreck, not a force. Breaking havoc, call me
havoc because I am not queen- like when I
am insane. I lose my sense of Queen-ship
when I am not sane. Flipping, twisting my*

neck, and clapping my hands to let you know I'm no game.

Do not dare correct me and try to check me, not while my temper is red hot. When I calm down, Jekyll & Hyde, is that you over there? Yes, you heard me. Good & crazy. However, I'm learning that good & crazy is only acceptable to those that are good & crazy along with you. So, I stopped being crazy so that I could be good.

Chapter Two

A Conversation with Self

I said, do not be consumed with outer beauty. Be consumed with inner beauty. There is no concealer or foundation to cover ugly motives, and intentions. Forgive yourself, forgive others. Respect yourself and put God even before yourself. With God in your life, you will genuinely Learn Self-love, Self- care, Dignity, Self-Respect, Honor, and Loyalty. Just put him first. I have realized just how unprepared I was for relationships and how I felt that being in a relationship made me feel worthy, beautiful, stronger, and more accepted. I might have made poor decisions; you may have too. However, there is redemption. There is still hope to become a better, stronger, more beautiful you without the validation of a man or woman. The reality is, for certain things in life, we are just not ready.

"Beauty Starts in Your Head Not the Mirror."

Joubert Botha

SIS

IS

NOT

READY

Trapped Walls

Little Girl!

Grown Woman's body. Send the Antidote
to save me from another body. Numbers
add up when frustration adds up trying to
keep my head up. Emotions fucked up,
time to knuckle up.

Past Pains, hardly anyone to blame.
Things aren't even the same. Half of me
want to change my damn name. I need a
cure to go back to being sane.

Being pure. Maybe a hand in my hand just
to be sure. Who's here? Just me? Oh, It's
just me?

People flee, and time is of the essence.

I used to get in God's presence. I need to get in God's presence. He gives you power when you lay prostrate.

Figure It Out

I'm in agony. I'm restless! Restless with nowhere for my aching soul to go. My mind is doing flips and trips and I'm in padded mental rooms. Who can rescue me now? My home girls are worn out and family too. Another boo won't do it because he'll just leave. The moment he figured me out. My bullshit that is. So, who's going to do it. I'm the same Self - destructive, Overspending, Overeating, Overly indulging, Masturbating, Even with people in the room, Lonely Chic. I said I feel like I can't win. Who's here now? But me! See now I got to deal with myself. No sense in trying find another human. It's time to figure my shit out. I am lost because I didn't want to be found. Angry, because I wouldn't let go. I am confused, because my first mind isn't good enough. I need more validation.

What do you think I should do? Oh, what you think I should do? Instead of looking up to God and asking, Lord, what do you think I should do?

The truth of the matter is we are all trying to figure our shit out. So nobody has time for the insecure adult on crutches. It's time to get healing so I can walk.

Sometimes My Lust Is Stronger Than My Faith

Sometimes my lust is stronger than my faith. I'm not just talking about my sexual desires, but all that I desire. It's like a monkey on my back. I don't feel good till it's released. I don't feel good, till my soul has been snatched from me. Damn! My lust is sometimes stronger than my faith. I want to please God on deeper levels. Higher heights, and deeper Dimensions, but even while I pray it rides me, thoughts! Clit stimuli is important to me. It sets me free, for a moment. I chase those moments in need of a fix, I don't know if this needs to be fixed or if it's normal. My prayers go up, God see me, hear me, release me, but in the next moment I want my back arched and my stress to be released while my legs are up, till I can't see my feet or the ground beneath me. Soul snatchers! I wish it wasn't only about the climax, but now lust takes me on a ride I'm begging God to save me from. It steals my focus, leaves me broken. I mean damn, sometimes my lust is stronger than my faith. It seems that I can't conquer it. I'm more than a conqueror, but only to things I don't like. I mean I love. How can I conquer when I enjoy being conquered? I'm submissive to it. I've begged for it, convinced myself I need it, I want it, it calls me, and I go running, like it's God, I mean its God. Is it my God?

Have I chosen the saliva of my urethra over my creator? Damn! I'm lost. I mean I'm confused. I want him, but I want him. God I'm talking about, but lust I'm begging for. They say I got to fight daily to kill my flesh, but I'm not there yet. I want my flesh to win, it feels good. Too damn good. Damn! Sometimes, my lust is stronger than my faith.

BACK THE HELL UP

This nigga

Depression

Trying to run up on me,

I had to force 'em to back up off me.

Prayer so far

From my lips,

Smokey mirrors,

I'm touching with my fingertips.

Life is a trip,

Shit I'm trying To Catch a grip so I don't
trip and Bust my lip with self -destruction.
To God be the glory.

I'm,

Still,

Standing,

No pills,

Just

GOD'S MUSCLE,

and the memory of my grandmother

fussing

me out for

feelings to quit.

Brings tears to my eyes.

However,

I'm not going to let

This mess

Be My Demise.

Eyes Wide Shut

Your walk, your talk, your everything is so hood. You talk shit about me, but when were together, you act like we're understood. Lied to me and everything, what is it that I see? Blinded by your honey? Your words are like glaze ham, only leaving me feeling empty. Shit, you got the potential to be a pimp. The way you move fast and drop me like the past, but without the cash, because you are broke and I am broke, but your cumming makes me feel rich. You don't look for my climax; I guess that is just too hard. So, I say what is it do I see? Or is it your words that are like honey to me?

Your High

 I hate the come down from your high. It's nothing but fast rides, whiplash from my neck being whipped fast. Wishing I had a blast, that could last from your amusement park. I'm only left with the ache of my stomach, a twitch in my neck, and feelings of not again. Shit I hate the ride in your amusement park, but excited when I am in the park. I hate the come down from your high.

That Ratchet Shit

So, I write rhymes to cleanse my mind of the times I threw fits, tripping off dick. Shit that probably belongs to some other chic. But no suspense or surprise they weren't down for the high tides that would come anyway. I need to let God have his way. Funny how I run to religion like its meat for starving children, When I don't get my way, I want to play, forget to pray. I'm going to start calling them Sensei for all the lessons that have been coming my way. Bitch wax on and wax off. Used to let 'em define me like there was no substance inside me. Killing my pride. Now I offer myself an apology. But there is a brawler in me that won't quit. Queen's part seas. Can you see God Resting in my bosom? Long time coming, blessings, and longevity coming. Call me super bad. I am on my Mclovin.

Self- Destruction Anonymous

Hi, my name is Sami and I'm an addict. I just want to know, is the healing of the soul really real? Can I be made whole with the manifestation of peace? Leaving behind all the Dons that entered me? They left me feeling like a corpse. I'm so empty inside, and yet I'm still waiting like a widow for yet another don to come and penetrate, so I can breathe. It's not even fresh air, but I don't care. It's toxic but I won't dare leave it. They say there's freedom in death, so if my heart loses its beat from the dagger of him admiring another woman over me I say let it be. Even though it's not about the sex for me, I'll take any means of compassion, excuse me, affection, the touch of other Humans are drugs for me. I'll stay weak. Yes, I said it. I'll stay weak, just to feel alive for the moment. I become mental, caged in padded rooms with no windows when alone. I can't stand what it feels like to be alone, because I'm ugly inside. The scars are fresh, and the scars, are raw. I cannot bear to look at them, I can't even touch them. Anyone gets close I'll holler, but like I said it's only mental. So, I don't bother addressing it. Instead, I dress it. Keep my hair nice and buy things according to the ticket price. Oh, I walk with a glide like everything's alright, but when alone, I yearn to be filled like a urn with a body of ashes. Filled with old memories, dead dreams. Which I can't seem to get over. I take one to face, not a blunt, but maybe I should. Instead, I swallow his testicles like they say a real woman should. Just to make 'em feel good, and me too. He validates me. Him telling me how good I am. My heart skips a few beats. Slows down when he withdraws himself from me. Then I die another death. Somebody roll out the expensive casket. Even in death

*I'm vain. I would hate to be in something
cheap while I'm in pain. They say journal
and perhaps therapy? But I say is it
helping me?*

*To get help you have first come to terms
with, yes, it is me, I have a problem, my
name is Sami, oh I mean Christina and I'm
self - destructive and it has a strong hold
over me. Oh, don't forget Sami to
acknowledge a power greater than
yourself. That's the only way you're going
to get help. I ask, does this shit work? For
the hurt? I sabotage everything, and I
can't quite figure out why. I wreck my
brain with fancy ideology, overthinking,
oh and I'm trying prayer with consistency.
Man, I just want to know Is the healing of
the soul really real? Can I be made whole
with the manifestation of peace? Leaving
behind all the dons that entered me?*

*For right now, I'm just not ready to face
my ugliness so I'll just stay safe in this
padded mental room and die a thousand
deaths until I'm strong enough to rescue
myself.*

Hi, my name is Sami, I'm still an

addict,

and

I'm

still

suffering.

Chapter Three

"We Encounter Many Defeats,

But We Must Not Be Defeated."

Maya Angelou

The Serenity Prayer

God Grant me the serenity to accept the things I cannot change; Courage to change the things I can; and the wisdom to know the difference. Living one day at a time, enjoying one moment at a time, accepting hardship as a pathway to peace. Taking as Jesus did, this sinful world as it is, not as I would have it. Trusting that you will make all things right. If I surrender to your will so that I may be reasonably happy in this life. And supremely happy with you forever in the next Amen.

I'm learning to trust God with not only my problems, but all of me. I chose the Serenity Prayer as a guide for me to learn how to let go.

I've always had a problem with letting go of what I couldn't control. Now, I have entrusted my higher power with all of who I am, all of who I'm not, and all Who I want to be. I'm also learning how to trust God and let it go.

SIS

PRAYS

Love Unspoken

So, I decided to love me. I'm not bad you see, my heart has been broken, broken to pieces, but I still find a smile. A smile to drive all men wild, but my creator said: Don't look for it in man. Don't look for validation in man. I've already approved you. Your childhood might have bruised you, maybe even confused you, but you're mine, designed so fine and being complicated is just fine. Brown eyes and brown skin, lips full divinely carved for any lipstick. I didn't make them to wrap around some man's long extremity but made thick to utter words of sweet nothings to me in the morning. To thank me for creating you. It was called power when I thought of you, I named you. Named you queen, I named you beauty and all others uniquely the same. Don't let anyone cause you to walk, eyes low and

shoulders sunken in. But instead stick your
chest out and walk with clout, because
you're mine the most high, almighty
divine.

Won't Let You Steal My Shine

Depression trying to close me in, and the pressures of life want to fold me to no end, but I'm not going to let it. I'm still going to shine. Even though I want to scream at the top of my lungs from all the frustration and deliberation between myself and myself, I'm just going to cast my imaginations down. It's time that I am free. Free from the inner me that doesn't feel worthy. Free from the inner me that's guilty and undeserving. The truth of the matter is, Yes, I hurt, but I matter, I don't always do right, but I'm worthy and I might not always get chosen by Mr. "All the girls want him," because we think he's it. But I'm enough. Yes, you heard me, I'm enough. God said so when he picked me. I was dirty with sharp thorns with torn petals and a withered stem, but he still wanted me. Yes, I'm broken, but I can be mended. Broken Rose! But make sure you call me, Ms. Through rich soil, I'm going to shine, I'm aging like fine wine, with the stamina of a teen and wisdom of a woman that's been redeemed. I said I can conquer it all. With God on my side, I can walk through invisible walls, and kill depression with the sword of my mouth. I can do this. I said, I can do this. I'm built for this, built to last, built with class and guess what? No, I can't rewind time, but I'm damn sure going to shine. God's guaranteed to give me what's mine, because I didn't quit. So don't you either. Just like granny's silver China, I'm going to shine. Like I'm polished, shine like the devil never tried to demolish me.

You can't break me or steal my shine; victory is already mine and it's about time I stand up for what's mine.

You Still Don't Get It!

As I sit here, in my chair with my heels high and my self- esteem low, feeling entitled to be in constant catty mode. I heard a voice in my ear say, "You still don't get it!" All the while you were crying, screaming, and calling my name I was there. Don't you get it? It hurt me to watch you feel agony, but it was for the benefit of my people. It was for the benefit of me, that you suffered. See anytime I allow a struggle, A storm, a calamity of any kind and I bring you out. It's an opportunity for you to help someone else come out. Don't you get it? Don't you know WHO I AM AS YOUR GOD?

As your healer, as your provider, as your confidant, as your battle ax, as your friend, your comforter, as your redeemer, as a bridge over troubled waters. When you look in the mirror don't you see me?

Hear me!

I keep my promises, have I left you? Have I forgotten you? I will never leave you nor forget you.

Why?

Because

I'm God.

God Asked, "How much do you love me?"

My Voice: *The other night you asked me, how much do you love me? You know That kind of baffled me. We have had this discussion so many times, and I've cried real tears, till my $25 eyelashes were dripping wet and I confessed how much you mean to me. How could you not know? I expressed how I appreciate all the times you have rescued me, patched up my broken heart, and when I would be falling apart, you would stitch each side closely together so it would leave no scar. You put me in a position to get a victory when I was losing. So I can get a win time and time again.*

*I do not know how, but somehow you
knew how to mend all the broken pieces,
even the regions of my brain that
developed mold from all the old residue,
the way back when in pain, that would
cause me to fold and crawl in the fetal
position, you somehow fixed all of that.
Even the times you provided when I had so
much lack. And I am not just talking about
financial means, but all the needs I needed
that my parents forgot to give or even
when they dropped the ball, you caught it
before I even hit the floor.*

How could you think I do not love you?

I call on you time and time again. You're obviously the seasoning to my meat, the syrup to my dark pancakes, and the reason I'm able to beat my feet in the streets. Even on Sundays, I press my way when I'm tired just so we can meet, but yet you question my love for you? But can't you see? I talk to people constantly about how much you mean to me. I tell them that you are a miracle worker, you are a friend indeed and you are a rider for every need and a companion, a multiplier of every seed. It's not just about money, but everything you plant sprouts to greater and everything you put your hands to, it becomes better. I tell them how I depend on you more so than a man. I know you hear me. You had to see how

I fed the homeless man good food, not just a burger from McDonald's, but Stew chicken with rice and peas from the Jamaican spot. I treated him just how you treat me around the clock. So, what will it take for you to see? I even was abstinent, no sex for a couple of years for you. Yeah, I went back on my word, but you know I am not perfect, but my effort should've been worth it. Do you hear me? Are you listening? Answer me!

Do you know what he said?

God's Voice: *Ok, daughter, are you ready to listen? Yes, you've cried real tears, and I collected them, I loved you so much I rejected them. The ones who had bad intentions and wanted to use for their gain and cared less about the pain you felt. What about the time I rocked you to sleep when you were too numb to feel, and even when you wanted to end your own life, I was there to see that you made it home that night. I am not like a man that I would throw my blessings in your face, but sometimes as humans your mind somehow erases all the love I have shown and all the blessings that've been thrown your way, even things you didn't even think of to ask for. What about the time you were abstinent? Come on, let's talk about it! I healed you, and you promised that you would not look back, but as a matter of fact, you broke your promise and ran back when things got hard. You claimed that you were in this for the long haul, but even though I knew that was a lie, I still rewarded you. Faithful and true. I have kept my word. I have never left you. I protected you because you were not ready. So yes, answer this one question. How much do you love me? I need to know. You have not obeyed my commands or do anything that I have asked because you want to do your own thing, and I am about growth, and you just want to stay the same. You asked how can I not know? You love me. Well, when are you going to commit? "Choose ye this day whom you will serve." You or me? But choose quickly, because I will not be standing here long, waiting to hear the answer.*

Again, how much do you love me?

I Wish We Had the Answers

Damn, I don't even know what to say. Life is strange the way it decides our growth. We do not get to choose when the lessons will be taught or how many battles we will win. With so many twists and turns, I cannot even say I've learned all that it's taught. Half of the time it goes so fast, we do not even catch our wind, but I am sorry for your loss. Even though you have gained, you've gained another level of maturity and a profound existence of understanding. What is this thing called life? I am not sure, but if I asked death, it would probably say, think twice, because we might not be able to make the same decision twice. I pray that you find closure in this opened door.

May you receive healing and abundance from all love you are receiving and much more.

May you be granted peace and freedom in chambers of your heart that were handcuffed and barely hanging, trying not to fall apart. I wish we had the answers.

Or maybe we do. It is this thing we call life. It's strange, but it decides our growth, but we decide what we do.

Just When You Thought It Was Over

They say time heals all wounds, but that's not true. It happens when understanding meets you. It is at the intersection of hope & despair. Kind of like "breathe again" street. It is not by choice, because sometimes the pain takes away our continuous heartbeat, but then a superpower meets our natural and then we get our second wind. It is not about a life of past sin, where you have been, or how many times you let your flesh win, but it is an opportunity to experience. It is not until we have lost that we can experience a true win. Some of us have been chosen to deliver others from pain that might have taken them out, but we have been assigned the task to go through and in return go back and help others cross over too. After all the why Me's?

How could you let this be? God, I thought you loved me, after the tears and the countless empty bottles of sin we have chosen to drown in. There we meet her. We see her standing there, brave, with strength like a cheetah. Just when we thought we would not make it. It happens. We meet understanding at the intersection of hope and despair. Kind of like "breathe again" street. It is not by choice, because sometimes the pain takes away our steady heartbeat. This time we got our second win. Braver with the strength like a cheetah and this time ten toes down, standing tall on our feet, and it is a victory that we conceive.

I have never seen you hurt so Severely

I have never seen you hurt so severely before. I know no one could prepare for a pain so great. I assure you she is great. While she is greeted by the angels and presented with her new body, walking around the streets of Gold. She cannot even imagine wanting to come back, but she will wait for you. She will wait, just like you, to reunite. Then y'all can catch up and she can show you around that vast place, and introduce you to mysteries untold, everything that our creator withholds. I have never seen you hurt so intensely before, and I know no one could prepare for pain so great, but I assure you she is great. While she is greeted by the angels and presented with her new body, walking around the streets of Gold.

This kind of hurt no one can take away. Only God can soothe it. So, I pray he rocks you to sleep, and continues to carry you when you feel weak. May he comfort you with the memory of the good old days. The long talks will remain in your heart. Guess what? You get to cherish a sisterhood that some could only fantasize of having, that you were blessed to share at least once in this lifetime. We do not know why God chose this way, but I pray that he gives you peace with his decision, and may he continue to push you into his purpose for your life. So, you can leave your mark in this world, with all of your people, just like she did.

Rapture OF Love

He whispers in my ear, Erasing all darkness and fear. Fluorescent light shining bright. It is all good tonight. Wondering if I could ever see the day, for sure now, for he is the potter, and I am the clay. For he cares for me, now I can see. Let my hair swing and feel the breeze. Look! I am a new me, no more chains holding me. Predicated on my reality. I could have never beat this or kick that, let alone stopped the road on that self-destructive track. Oh, but with faith, with faith I can see. I can see all that is not even yet in front of me. Unlike mortal man, he has never cheated or even lied to me, and when I am with him it is about me. For he loves me and cares for me. Promised he would never leave or forsake me. There is no shame when he holds me. I am glad he chose me. No longer am I weak. My lover calls me strong, and respected. Not afraid of the future for he holds the future in his hands. So, from this moment and forever more I will be the woman he has called me to be. Speak and walk as he has birthed me. In my new mind he has made me whole. I sing new songs to rhythm and blues not losing control. I once depended on a man, but Sistas no man could do it. Now, I stand boldly, proud of who I am, what I can do and all that I can stand. He chose me. He is my lover, and I am his. So, the next time somebody asks you when was the last time you smelled roses or had some beautiful lilies on your table? You tell them, baby, I am a lily. Picked uniquely from his garden.

Devotion

*So, I do not look at my friends when I am
going through, but I cry out to you. I lift
my hands to you. See, no one knows me as
you do, and no, it is not about cars, houses,
having a man, or better yet, provoking
you to do things to see if you got a plan.
Even though you do. I do not treat you like
a piñata, taking a bat, beating you to the
max, to get more and more out of you.
That is a fact, but what we have is true
blue, I am not going to use you as my
pimp. Forget to leave an offering, oh, and
when I do, it is just a tip. Dollar or two,
then treat you like a clown, want you to
perform like you just came into town. No,
no, this is not a circus. I am through, tired
of the same old hocus pocus, artificial love,
leaving me broken. I lift my hands,
knowing that I will not be the same,
because with you, all things are never the
same, but new. So, I leave my blues at*

your footstool. My girlfriends will not do, and another boo will just make me lose. I stay true and give you praise and stay loyal, Down for you. Oh, and I'm going to raise my son to love you too.

Poetry is my Spear

I have risen from death with written repentance. I am sorry, In so many words. Guilt has beaten me to a pulp. I do not recognize my spirit. It is raw. I find that poetry is my spear though, it resuscitates me. It Circulates my blood, palpitates my heart, restoring brain function. I have died a million times, but spilled ink did it for me.

Yet again! I mean I have beaten myself enough. I forgive myself for not being perfect. For not doing things without mistakes. Aren't I here for mistakes? It is not like I lived life before. So how would I know? Shouldn't I be easier on myself?

Instead, I have used my tongue to cut deep like my kitchen knife. Poetry is my spear, though.

*It keeps me breathing; After I have been
used up, these bruised words become life.
They become strong. Cotton in my mouth
becomes saliva, and yet I form words that
I could not utter at once.*

*With the same mouth I have destroyed, I
have given life, even to others. Poetry, I
carry in my heart. Rhymes a million times,
make space on lines. I could write you a
parable, but I prefer poetry because it is
my spear. It is my rhyme and reason. It is
my life. It dismantles demons in the night,
it dismantles self- destruction, the enemy
in me is exposed when I open my mouth.
Should I call it my machete? Or my spear?*

*Either way, it is lacerations are deep, not
easily sealed, covered, or even protected. I
am not here to play, I am not here to tickle
your fancy, this right here is raw, it is real,
it is life or death. If I do not write,*

*I will not be right. It is a fight, my
personality splits at times, with strain to
put pen to paper, but I will not be lazy,
because poetry is my spear. It is my life!*

Chapter Four

A Conversation with Granny

Granny said, most of us do not raise our sons to be hurtful, but sometimes, they turn out that way. There are some good men. However, beware of the ones that talk sweet to you to get into your panties. Establish your own emotionally and physically and if they leave, you will be able to stand on your own two feet. You do not want to be a woman that cannot do anything for yourself. Never, stop living, even if he leaves you. If you are striving to be a child of God, you should not be looking for fun, so be mindful of how you carry yourself. If you are a disciple of Jesus Christ, he will only allow but so much to happen to you. It is ok to think that, if it is going to happen it will happen but do not go around being reckless. It has been seventeen years since She has been free from Breast Cancer.

She learned all things are possible with Jesus Christ. She said, "Always love yourself." "If no one loves you, the Lord loves you and he sees things in you that you may not even see in yourself." "Who is greater than him?" Granny is 74 years old, and she has not seen much change in the world. However, she is grateful that all her children made it to adulthood and received their education. They were fortunate enough to establish themselves in the world. She has been married for 35 years and she advises people to get to know one another and try not to go to bed angry. She says, "Sometimes, people grow apart, but that's because they never knew each other."

"Knowledge Speaks

But Wisdom Listens"

Jimi Hendrix

SIS

IS

BECOMING

WISE

The Little Girl In Me Started Healing Today

The little girl in me started healing today. She awakened from death, the moment he said, that it was not her. He said that it was not him either. It was his parents, learned behavior, So I started healing today, knowing that it was inevitable, it is my cross to bear, and there is nothing else that can be done about it.

The little girl in me started healing today. I realized that the guilt I carried came from Satan, who used my mistakes to pound me out, he tried to decapitate my mind, but I am still here, I am still standing. I am healing today knowing that my mother meant no harm when she criticized me and made me feel like I was not good enough.

She was learning too. I had to unravel the layers to find that I am truly, Good enough. So, I started healing today. I am learning to forgive myself for those boys I let win, even from the devil I let in. I said, I let him in, so That makes me responsible. I am learning to let go of the past. I am learning to press and push and drive out darkness with love. I am learning to heal thyself. The Little Girl in me is healing today, knowing that I will never be perfect, but I am a masterpiece in God's hands. So, I have peace with that. The little girl in me is healing today.

Is God A Woman?

*The way we move our hands like the sway
of magic, baking and making that bread
making sure everyone is fed, I said is God
a Woman? We have turned water into
wine with little grapes. Manifesting
dreams of our dead ancestors and the ones
alive too. We, the black woman, are the
Great! Black! Hope! With dope running
through our veins, I am not talking about
no drug, but dope, as in Dominant,
Optimistic people, that Empower.
Uplifting to dimensions unknown. God
must be a woman the way omnipresence is
magnified, multitasking faster than
gentrification moves like plagues and
tsunamis, through the boroughs.*

*No, I am not saying God, has a gender, or
even the "white man" is up to his agenda,
but if we must, let us just say it must be a
woman the way things get done.*

This woman must be black the way she maneuvers through the universe with order and finesse. Do not ask for anything less than blessings. Oh she is a blessing all by herself. God is full of wisdom, so we know she wrote the proverbs, and God is full of verbs with actions that make relentless foot soldiers fall back. God is blameless, melanated, and shameless. Only a woman can turn sloppy mud into art fixtures of man and then send him to work. Yes, make money and bring it back home, provide for your home. Man will know how to earn his keep. God must be a woman. Can you hear me? Blueprinting, Constructing, and building. Sounds like a woman to me. Matchless, selfless, Undeniably, Incredible, and that is just the God in me.

One Mother

I came from one woman, but can I have more than one mother? Whether alive or gone, there can never be another. I mean I can have mother figures, mothers to mention and mothers with good intentions, but I will only have one mother. We only can be born of one woman. Naturally! I mean spiritually I have been assigned one too, but nothing will ever compare to the one that carried you. Some may beg to differ. Some natural mothers are only just that, natural. They pushed and they pushed, but could never push you into destiny, they could never push you to deeper dimensions. Maybe they have never gone themselves. I have learned that I can only have one mother. My spirit tells me that. When I am scared, lonely, my spirit yearns for that connection.

It is almost like it remembers a connection that I once had but lost. My spirit longs for something it had. I long for something stronger than crack. That is a mother's love. I want to be rocked and cradled, maybe even swaddled like newly born babies. To remind me of safety. I can only have one mother, but I have been looking for you in others, but I cannot find you. Nothing compares to the time we shared when I bonded with you. A connection so rare. Not even my father shared. However, we tell the story when you left or when I left, the bond was broken, and I have been left sulking! Leaking! Left in spiritual pieces. I mean the meaning of connection is meaningless. At night, when I long to be understood, I call my friends, waiting to hear a familiar sound, waiting to hear the voice my soul remembers, but there is no voice recognition. I search and search hoping to find you in another, just because we cannot get along. It is almost like we cannot stand each other. I promise, you will not find me in another, and I will not find you either. These diamonds are cut rare, and just like fingerprints I do not think another DNA that matches mine. It is almost like I need you. I need you to unlock the code to my insecurities and only you can tell me "it's going to be alright," and It will be. It is almost like, only you, my mother, can tell me "I'm just right," and I will believe it. So, no! No one will ever compare nor will I share another bond like ours. This one is rare. Even the devil likes to compare, because he tricks me with the same tricks he used to trick you. I guess we are the only ones that do not get it. Hopefully, we will learn and never forget it. We need each other to survive. I can no longer take pride and walk around like I do not need a mother; I say stupid stuff like, I am fine on my own, when I am

*walking the earth alone. I have lost my
womb connection, and I have tried looking
for you in others, but now I know, I will
never find you in another, because I only
have one mother.*

Fearless

I do not have any more time for foolery, I said have no time for grudges, malice, and trickery. Corona came to claim my life. My heart was not right; Life hit differently when that fever spiked. Now, I pray that the Lord pass me not, be a gentle savior. Breathe again, on my son too. You are the only one that can save us. Funny how we know to bow down, when it is out of our control, funny how we know to bow down when we are about to fold, but that was my last time putting God 2nd, 3rd, or 4th. He is not no has been, no Phony or no flake, nor is he an option, he is my choice, so I surrender my heart, my whole heart, I am not holding nothing back, and you will get all I got. Besides, what other reason did you not let Corona claim me. What other reason am I here for? What other reason did you save me?

Purpose

I have been chosen to wait. Wait till the perfect time. So, I'm waiting, or should I say I'm building. Time has chosen me to wait and contemplate today, for tomorrow is not promised. Though I may not be ready, time is pausing to catch me up to speed, and it waits for no one, but it chose me, to wait. Am I special? No, I am just chosen, chosen to unlock purpose. I must make haste to learn necessarily while I yet stand still and build. Building to make me better, not to gain a man, but to gain myself. It is senseless to chase the black woman's dream in a man. While he is yet fighting the black man's plight for his rights. Not only America but our brothers and sisters compete to some degree. Is that healthy? It is not by chance or coincidence that I have been chosen, and it is not to boast. It is to manifest a power that is locked inside of me and you. To bring forth discovery in us. My purpose is not selfish. My purpose is not greedy. My purpose is not contingent on anyone else, but me. But God. My purpose is to ignite fire inside of you. When I am set free, you will feel the breeze too. When I'm successful, you will gain space to live, laugh and own too. The system of purpose is not about even just you or me. It is about us. Purpose is fulfilled when we are divinely connected, equally yoked at the hip. This wait is not for willy- nilly or silly endeavors. It is for fertilizing, incubating, and birthing. Understand this! When you die, and you have not used the gifting inside of you, purpose has died. What other reason are we born? But to be fulfilled.

Love Is

*I said, self! Don't you know that you are a
queen? I said it before, but I mean it this
time as I say it again. My brown lips will
not be entered to fill thrills and the spill of
his semen will not delight my vulva nor
will my heart feel conditions of beatings
over and over. I'm good this time. I said I
have learned this time. That my queenship
does not involve childish pursuits of
daddy's love in honey, big and thick. I do
not need my legs open, to fill love and
make him open. However, my mind will do
that. I said I have learned this time. That
sex will not win him, but my mind will do
that. First, I will win "myself." Now that
my heart is split open, I know what love is.*

*I know what it feels like. Love is when I
lick my wounds, patching myself up again.
Love is the gentle touch.*

It is not in pounding myself out over yet another fall, but when I use the time God gives me alone to learn how useful it is to be alone. It is not in my tears or sentiments of words that my homegirl gives. Yes, she loves me when she says, "bump that." "You can do better." No, it is not in that, but love enters me like an awaited consummation. When I say bump that, I will do better. I will love who I am and not look for another to do it for me. I cried real tears this time, but it was not only because he left me, but it was because I left me, like I was left waiting in the living room for him to get me. I was sitting there with my coat on. When I was seven, it is years later, but I am still seven. I still do not think I am worth it, but I vow to myself, I will not drag myself by my locs again, not with this same sin. I am done with this torture. I cannot get used to this.

I mean I am numb to him penetrating my heart, then penetrating my love parts, and then giving me his ass to kiss. You know, the same way I do myself. I deserved to be loved. I deserve to love myself finally.

I Am More Than A Label

I learned today that labels are not who I am. Sounds cliché, and no, there is nothing wrong with a brand here and there, but I will not be broke anymore, just to walk down the street with confidence, with swag, and let my clothes brag. Nah, I am on my new shit. My denim does not need to be designer to be official when I am already Ms. Official. The war scars that I have gained from the switch, that is my tongue, talking nothing, but negativity. Telling myself how that was dumb, Over, and over again. Buyer's remorse, and the designers have no remorse. I feel like they make clothes with expensive price tags especially for me. While they are designing, they may be thinking of my insecurities. Or maybe it is just me.

It is almost like they know they will gain more wealth, because I do not think wealth. I mean, I do not think I am worth it unless I have it. They just sit back and laugh at it. They would not even do it. They would not even buy a T-shirt that is $100 plus just because somebody's name is on it. They won't even buy J's to say they own it. They invest that same bread and flip it like a street hustler. The difference is they will not do time because it's not considered a crime to prey on the weak. Shit the minute I buy, I arrest myself. Putting myself in bars of the labels. The thought of it makes me sick, but now my eyes are open. It is never too late to respect money, and my purpose does not come in dark blue denim with shredded holes in it. I remember a time when once jeans got holes in 'em we didn't want to wear them. Now, we buy them because somebody said this is the style now. The earn for the *almighty dollar is just too hard to spend senselessly. I am changing my thinking from being a laborer punching clocks, only to buy a couple of items and be stuck with lent pockets. Dammit, I refuse to have to pay the IRS and the almighty designers. I'm staying in my lane, I am on my new shit.*

I'm Ready

I'm ready! To walk and glide on this pavement. To speak the truth and live it. To regurgitate all the lies I made my dwelling place. I am ready to cut the ties of childhood and become a whole woman. No more am I broken, bound, and Barron. My womb bears fruit, no more desolate places. I am free. Free from rejection. I have cut the ties between them and me. Now, I can shake loose those filthy rags of deception. Those rags are too small. I have grown past self- destruction. I have grown past not appreciating corrections. I said I am free, and readiness is not a feeling. It is my adjective. No longer addicted to fruitless endeavors and senseless pain. I said I am ready!

Ready to walk in the fullness of life, the splendor of my savior. No more is penis my savior, or should I say, my downfall.

I am made tough at heart, which qualifies me to be ready. Now I walk with my head up, no more shame or moderate self-esteem being a dream. I love me. I appreciate myself, so now I can move forward. Yes! I have finally passed the test. I know what love is. It is when I lick my wounds and nothing else. I do not need a pat on my back from him. My reward is the gain of self. I have won. My broken pieces are being glued back together again. My potter is diligently putting me back together again. So now, I can stand proud and say, I Am Ready.

The SistaHOOD

Shout out to the Sistahood for helping me get through the toughest time of my life. The Sistahood that does me good, by lifting me, rolling up their sleeves, getting their manicures dirty, in that sloppy mud I call my past. Pulling my arms up to get over mountains, my childhood hurdles, traumas, and no, there is no one to blame. We all go through it just the same. However, I owe a special thank you, to the Sistahood, that does me well, when you say, "Sis you are enough." You are not always dressed to the Tee, but you are good enough to be around me, you do not have to look fly and put together all the time. It is your insides that matter.

You are not always right, however, you are right for the right one. The Sistahood!

I love you when you are broke, I love you when you are wealthy, I love you, even when you do not love yourself properly. Do not worry, I am going to nurture you to good health. I am going to mother you in the areas that you still need mothering. Yes, we all still need mothering. I got you because I am your Sista and your mine. It is not always your fault, and yes, sometimes you get on my nerves when you do things I do not like, but it is alright, because you are not perfect, and I'm not perfect, But we're Sistas. I love you. I am here to remind you that you are the gift that keeps giving. When God created you; He created good seed. Planted good seed, that births bridges over troubled waters. In your hands, there is healing. In your hands, there is deliverance. In your hands, there's millions of inventions, completed tasks, provisions, and in your mouth, there is life. In your mouth is love.

In your mouth lies a defibrillator. When you speak a word to me, I rise from my bed of affliction, like Lazarus, when Jesus said, "Come forth." You help me conquer my Goliath, and those giants come tumbling down, when you give me hard, meaningful love.

You know just when to be gentle, but you know just when to give it to me straight, no chaser. Even then, you still know how to add a little ice to water it down. The Sistahood! Thank you, for breaking things down when I am too stubborn to understand. You are teaching me how to speak with love in different languages, not just my own. I am grateful to you all. My Sistas. It is not always a brother that will help heal you, Sometimes, and almost most times it is your Sista. When she is not using her tongue to kill you, but building up, Not competing with you to outdo you, but uplift you, and not sleeping with your *man behind your back, that's wack, and unacceptable. Sistahood, is not for the faint. It's for those that choose to endure. The Sistahood!*

Chapter Five

"Pour Yourself A Drink,

Put on Some Lipstick and Pull

Yourself Together."

Elizabeth Taylor

Conversation with The Council

(*A Group of Women who are older and wiser than you*)

What does self- love look like? I could not quite figure out what love for myself would be like. It was scary. It was embarrassing not to have already loved myself. I was ashamed to say, I do not love myself. Sometimes, I do not even like myself. However, I knew what flirting with myself was like. I often flirted when looking cute. The minute I did something painful to myself, like sleeping with men for validation, for love, for esteem, I would then fall from the grace of potential love from self. Then I would not be flirting with myself anymore. I would fall into self-hate, dislike, and torment. Browbeating became a norm. I ask again, what does love for myself look like? Is there a sound that comes from my mouth? Is there a glide in my walk? Is there something that I should do to resonate with the action word "love"? I wondered if other women had the same questions I had, or whether they were going through the same journey as I was. The thing that I thought to do was, seek counsel from a group of women that I trust with whose opinions I value and trust. Women that are wiser than I and have lived and survived things that all women will go through at some point in their journey. They explained to me that love is not INSANE. To love myself I had first to change my thinking. I had to acknowledge that I could no longer continue patterns of abuse upon myself. They also explained to me that I had to decide to stop doing the same things over and over, again which caused me pain. I have learned from them that love is FORGIVENESS. I felt that I deserved to feel pain. I believed that I deserved to suffer for my transgressions. The guilt of my past would not allow me to be free,

even after God set me free by being the truth. He set me free by laying down his life on a cross for my sins. However, when guilt would arrest me, Jesus dying for me was not good enough. That is what my actions said, when I would not let go of the guilt, the pain, and the transgression. I had to physically and mentally let go of my transgressions and the guilt holding me hostage. I had to let go of bondage. I am learning to get rid of everything connected to the bondage as well. In my pursuit for wholeness, I have gone to religious retreats, church, spoke with friends, and elders, but it never resonated with me that I first had to learn that love is ACCEPTANCE in me. All that I am and all that I am not. Accepting that I am not perfect, I am right for the relationship with myself and others. I will never be perfect. I will make mistakes, and fall, but it is in my getting up that counts most.

Acceptance is my key to loving myself. My sisters have told me that love is ENOUGH. I am enough. I do not need to over-compensate to be loved, or to befriended or to be happy. My smile, my laugh, my appearance, my views, my stature, poise, and all. It is all ENOUGH. I do not need to be something I am not or be like someone else to be liked or loved. I AM ENOUGH and I am BEAUTIFUL just AS, I AM. I am learning that love is PATIENT and UNDERSTANDING. I had to instill in myself that love is being patient with my growth. Being patient with my healing process. The damage was not done overnight, neither will the healing process be done overnight. It takes time to unravel the layers. It takes time to tap into deeper levels of understanding. A wise person once told me, "To be understood I must offer understanding." I have learned that there's grace in understanding.

Understanding helps with forgiveness. Forgiveness helps with being and feeling free. There's Grace in loving ourselves for real. Now that I am walking in this revelation, I am learning what it takes to consider myself GROWN.

SIS

IS

GROWN

Sick Folk Can't Rescue

I must admit, I wanted them to reach down with their keys of purpose and unlock doors of those generational curses that have been beating me non- stop to a pulp. I purpose you to heal me. I wanted all of you to speak to those dry places while lying Intimately, and wipe my tears with your laughs, and bring wrath to those who hurt me. In my mind, I purpose you for this task. It was not until I saw you were crippled too, that it was going to be difficult for you to put pieces of me back together again, because you do not recognize the word whole. I mean you yourself, cannot spell it out either. I figured we could sound the word out together. I purpose you for this. No, you did not die on a cross, or turn water into wine, but I figured you could turn my emptiness to completeness. See you were going to make me a whole person. I have been walking around split, with a split personality. One minute I am smiling, the next I am crying, one minute I am full of joy, the next full of shit. All of you were supposed to uncripple me, and I uncripple you. None of it really mattered to me that you could not spell whole, healed, set free or even knew the enunciation of deliverance. It did not matter to me, but my mind was set on making you the one. I wanted you to be the one because I was infatuated. Infatuated with the lust of my eyes. The stench of mistrust wore on me like silt from an everlasting fire. I needed to repurpose you. I had to fall on my face and realize in my disgrace, that sick folk can't heal me. Nor do we know how to rescue each other. Your brokenness of not having a father triggered my issues of "daddy did not do enough," your issues of lack of momma did not nurture you enough, triggered my issues of "insecurity." I was looking for you to mend my broken pieces, but you could not find yours. So, I am learning to lust less and pray more because sick folk can't rescue me.

I'm Tired, But I'm Good

Trying to regroup from the group that blasted me, not knowing I have another fast in me. For he is greater in me so I'm tired, but I'm good. Not so hood, but just enough, just enough, I said just enough to get through. Funny how I made it through, because the tides were high, and the wave was wild. Some may call it rough, so I got a little tired. Still good though. Wondering how many rounds it's going to be though. I'm sick and tired of the same fight just about every night. Encouraging myself with things like it's going to be alright. The weapon was not supposed to prosper, somehow feeling like I got hit. It's cool, a little blood, but I'll just change my shirt, It's nothing but a little dirt.

After this, I will put on my pencil skirt,
high heels, cute bangles, right arm just to
fill my thrill. No more Achilles Heel,
tormenting flakes, feet aches or flats. I'm a
little tired for now, but I'm still good.

I Am Enough

Malcolm X asked, "WHO TAUGHT YOU TO HATE YOURSELF?" So, I wear kinky locs to keep me from falling into a box of caged thinking. Before then I was asleep, knee- deep in insecurity, not knowing my capabilities. Complained about my beauty because I wanted to look like another from down the block. Around the clock, fantasies of what it would be to have a different- looking face, thicker legs, maybe long straight hair, Eyes with a prettier glare. All these misconceptions and crooked perceptions. They kept me from seeing the blessings that were bestowed upon me. Realizing there could never be another me, made distinctly, high cheekbones, breathing air through wide nostrils, dark brown eyes, Jawbone, strong, by no surprise. Fearfully & wonderfully made.

Through God's Eyes. So, I do not look to another race to keep up the pace, indirect messages sending direct messages that meet my pupils to try to generalize what a black woman should look like. Even though I was born in sin and shaped in iniquity, the power of God in me, pushes me to Godly expectations. I am breaking all limitations and warped thinking, I have been designed finely, like wine. My body looks right. My booty still matters, and it does not have to get any fatter for me to know my name, because I am lovable just the same.

Unapologetically Black

Pop. Pop. Pop. Pop. Every day my black skin is risky, every day my black skin can get me killed. There is no regard for black lives, so how can we matter? They force a mask on our face, but if We were a gang, we would have a case. America is the largest gang of 'em all. The largest murderers of em all, the largest bigots of em all, I said the largest bullies of em all, wonder where our children get it from. "The chickens have come to roost." They want to choke us out of a voice. Hoping that fear will rage and silence us until we have no voice, No say, Slavery in modern-day. I guess they care for our trees more than if we can breathe. Eumelanin DNA on Noose is not even outdated. We are still ornaments on trees, but we cannot be silenced. Our ancestors protest from graves and pits, blood shed from our backs

*and you want us to turn our backs. Capital
punishment for being black? "This power
we have, has conceded demand."
Mimicking our swag will not make you a
supporter. Wearing our clothes and
jamming to our musical culture will not
make you a part of our cause. You got to
fight, suffer and die like us. Eumelanin
cannot be mimicked, it got to be in you,
and I am not referring to black Mandingo
in you. This right here is true, and you got
to be black to walk a mile in my shoe.
America, we are not asking for you to heal
us. We are healing ourselves, every time
you hear NO JUSTICE! NO PEACE!
Our healing is taking root. Every Voice
lifted, we are overcoming your blues, so
no, and we do not need your pity, those of
you who are white, privileged, and silent. I
am talking to those of you who have ONE,
black, Friend. You cannot be quiet while
children are beaten for not wearing a*

mask, while we are killed for being black at last. They should be encouraged and taught, By ALL. We are not foolish. We will guide and reprimand our own. We do not need your black batons on our black skin to teach us a lesson. Your ancestors have done enough of that. We stand today, unapologetically, black.

Don't Get It Twisted

These eyes don't lie. They are full of pride in oneself. Oh, we are not just black women with beauty and hips, with a switch to make a man want to leave extra gratuity. We are brains with wit, eyes with 20/20 devising plans with vision. Even in our sleep our dreams are with precision. We can flip bricks without touching, build companies from scratch, count figures, owners, they want to match. Call us Ms. Cultivator. We develop even those that are gifted to create. We are the check in mate. Strategizing is our niche, kamikaze if you make us flip our switch, the bomb Dot Com. We can dap with the guys, but wine & dine at the same time. Red heels do us fine, and we're such ladies, knowing how to keep things in its perfect time. There is no neediness, or desperation in our eyes. We have tussled with relentless demons, so we are a force to be reckoned with.

Passing us around? Nah, we will not be

sloppy, second fiddled with. Self -control is

the coloring of our pupils. Can you see

deep within us? Our soul is clean because

We have pleaded with the Lord. Do not

come at us with any foolishness. Our eyes

are not misleading, with stones that were

thrown at us, we have rebuilt our temple.

So, do not misconstrue our ability because

of our anatomy, because these eyes don't

lie.

My Crown May Sometimes Slip

Don't just call me female but call me woman. My Crown may sometimes slip, but it will never fall off. My camel toe has power, but it is not the power I chose to use. My brain! Is the perfect tool. I move mountains with my tongue, my shadow causes imps to hide and run. Trouble does not live here anymore. When I raise my fist, it is not used to pound the face of some slick talking chic, but only raised to show unity & strength. I win wars with the bow of my knees, I can make demons beg and plead, and I am just that bad, but only because God resides in me. Now, I once thought that if I created plenty of saliva and appeased him sexually, I would have that queen-ish swag and will not have to buy my bags. Sadly mistaken, Queenship came when the X chromosome met the other X. So, I stop living lies and empower oneself. A raspy voice with three legs can only satisfy for a moment, but the thought process of it is me, that I need, lasts way longer. Every day moving forward, so yeah, sometimes my crown may slip, but it will never fall off.

Self - Made

*Here to disclaim there is no destruction
taken root, self- pity, or obstruction of my
justice, I'm living proof, you got to earn
your keep, there's nobody coming to the
rescue, I'm doing it. God's strength, I am
getting through it. Legacy is not going to
pave itself, but this road my fore-mothers
and my fore-fathers have mapped, I am
filling the gaps. The wedges in these
curses, I am dismantling, I will be free, I
shall be who God has made me. I was not
born to be in the shadows or walk around
so my little ass can make patty cake claps.
I am born black; resilience is my name,
and others born the same. So no, do not
call me typical. I am worth more than
acrylic nails, fly shoes we wear, exuding
finesse, I am built for the press, I produce
under heat, defecating diamonds, no scars,
I am passing this trauma.*

I am done with that "I'm not good enough" and "I'm not making enough money to do enough" attitude. I am fighting through. No dude riding in, on a white horse. There is no Prince charming with no, left behind, glass slipper. I buy my shoes. I said, I'm self- made. Using what God gave me to get to what I want; I'm writing to get what I want. Freedom! Free from my past. At last! I licked my own wounds, ten toes down, emotionally too, because I'm self- made.

I See Me

Now, that I have air I can breathe, breathe fresh air and tranquility. I see me being free. I see me full of laughter. I see me bossing up, but most importantly, I See Me.

Black woman,

Healer of self,

Fun,

Silly,

Smart,

Interesting,

Deep thinking,

Analytical,

Complicated,

Strong,

Wise,

Fighter,

Mother,

Daughter,

Sister,

Friend,

Daughter of Zion,

Mother of humanity,

HUMAN!

Student of LIFE!

Now that I have fresh air, I can breathe, breathe fresh air and have tranquility. I can see. I see me. Not the way others did, I do not look for their validation. I am free from popular opinion. I am free from the enemy in me. I will not self- destruct. I now know who I am. I have things to do. I do not chase men anymore. I see my value. I do not chase friends and family and want to be accepted. I see my value. I, see, ME. I asked God to show me who I am. Now that I know, I have air. I can breathe. I have tranquility. I Am Free. I, Am, Me.

Bow Down

I think you should bow down. I Heard 'em say the black woman is made in the image of God. With the power in our womb to contract the pain of a dying nation and bring forth new life of hope. Through wide mouths and voluptuous Lips, we feed knowledge and wisdom. Proclaiming truth to our youth. Please go ahead and sup from the nipple of Mother Earth and gain understanding. This black phenomenon is not only a black Areola, cracked, bleeding nipples. We breed diversity, amongst a land that do not know what to do with our gift. They do not quite get it, so they do not want it. So, they reject it, mortifying and killing it. We breed healing power through our hands because everything we touch gets resurrected and new strength. Birthing out fresh ideas, like God breathed life into the nostrils of Adam's nose, and resonates a movement like the sound of

Gabriel's trumpet except for this is not the end, yet!

Oh, go ahead and bow down to this melanated deity. By far, we are no Delilah so Samson you can go ahead and lie down in our lap. This woman is to be trusted. This is not just any typical juice- filled coloring with high fructose, but this is all- natural and exfoliating, real, truth, BLACK, GIRL, JUICE. We sit cool, full of peace and power, stamina that no man can devour. Do not even try to sleep with or creep with us.

This is not a fly- by- night. There's mystery in our thighs and wonders of the eclipse that lies between them. This, melanated Goddess. With full-faced features, hair of wool and skin of bronzes. Bow down when you meet us. You will be intrigued and beg not to leave us. I heard them say, the black woman is made in the image of God.

To Forgive Yourself

I forgive me for not loving me, the way I was supposed to, the way I was designed to, the way God intended me to. I forgive me for putting others before me like I never knew me. I forgive me for the torment of telling myself how I was not good enough, was not pretty enough, wasn't sexy enough, smart enough, talented enough. I said I forgive me for treating me like a chopped liver. I forgive me for settling for less than what I deserve, I even forgive me for punishing myself as I deserved, even after God gave me release. I said, I let it go, today, right now, this moment, my past is passed, the time has passed and there is nothing I can do about it, there is no restitution for the hurt, for the pain, for the sin. I am moving forward, I said I am released, and my past is deceased.

I'm free! I'm free! I'm free! I said I'm

RELEASED,

Because

I,

Forgive,

ME.

Today and right now.

A Diamond That Needs Buffing

I am full, not empty, blessed to be a blessing, finessed with God's grace, I'm walking mercy. Let these words abound with you as they do with me. I am birthed a female but mothered to be a woman. A diamond that needs buffing, cleaning, fire to my brim, carving those sharp edges, so that I do not cut you with my words. My words have the power to chop you down to filth, But I choose not to. I have been mothered enough not to. I said, my words can give you life, but they can also bury you in a grave you dig, be careful how you dig holes in me, I am still being buffed by my creator. Spit shined by the almighty. I am choosing to let him live in me. I have let niggas live in me. Rent free. Renting rooms in my mind, bringing his demons to play with mine, I wanted him to be mine, and indeed he is, his spirit, my spirit in twined, soul tied, we call it entanglement. Still full though, and it is not with crap. I have paid my dues for this. I have earned my beret for this, my general hat. Do not fix your mouth to devalue me. Do You know how long it took me to become a woman? Decades! I am still learning, it's not in my waist trainer, or my leopard suit that gives me strength to get through, but it's the truth that I spit from my heart, my mouth does not come with degrees unearned. I already told you, I paid for this. This Sista is not a thief. So, do not try me. Better yet, try me, and you will be slayed with this sword. Like 300. I am keeping it 100 and do not ever forget I am birthed a female and mothered to be a woman. A diamond that needs buffing, cleaning, fire to my brim, carving those sharp edges, so that I do not cut you with my words.

Here's A sneak Peak of my
Upcoming Book of Short Stories

#LESSONS

I wonder if I jumped, would my lungs collapse before hitting the ground. I need the pain to stop. How else will it stop? I'm so confused. (I pondered many thoughts) I prayed in my mind, God will you forgive me If I jumped? Please help me. Please, I'm begging you. As I walked in the building, these thoughts plagued my mind. Hello, I'm going to the twenty-second floor. "Ok," the security guard answered, "take the elevator on the right," as he pointed. I pressed the screen for the number of the floor I was going to and waited anxiously. The elevators are very modern now, for the year 2013, I guess you can call this Millennial age where everything is modernized and computerized. I waited nervously. I can't believe I want to kill myself. I'm really ready to end it all. How can I feel this way? Who's going to miss me anyway? I got in the elevator and anxiously pressed the number twenty-two. As the numbers appeared on top of the elevator wall, 15, 16, 17, 18, my heart palpitated like it was about to explode. I was shaking uncontrollably.

I looked down at my shaky, sweaty hands, with tears so heavy in my eyes, I could barely see the numbers are increasing. I thought of my family, my mother,. I knew I would be adding to her pain, my father would be greatly disappointed, and my friends probably wouldn't understand why I made this decision. I just can't take any more pain. My thoughts were uncontrollably racing. As I approached the twenty -second floor, my body was shaking, the elevator door opened, and I strolled down the hallway, still contemplating jumping. "Hi Riley, are you ok?" "Why are you going towards the staircase?" "The office is this way." As she pointed towards the opposite direction. I could barely speak, I just nodded my head in an upward way, to say I was ok, but I wasn't. Today is my therapy appointment; However, I decided to use this opportunity to go to the roof, being that it's always unlocked due to the mistake or mishap of the custodian. They say mental illness is a severe thing, but I'm not ill. I'm just going through something.

My therapist, receptionist, is a beautiful person, inside and out. She was in the hallway coming from the bathroom as I was walking down the hallway towards the staircase. The door to the roof had been unlocked during prior visits. I was curious to see how the staircase looked, and just so happened to look during other visits, just being nosey. When you've seen one staircase, you've pretty much seen them all. Could she have been my guardian angel? Her voice was soft -spoken, a little high -pitched, but not squeaky. Ms. Janice was always dressed for the gods. Nails done, hair done, everything done. Red bottom heels, classy pant suits, tailored at the ankle. Even her perfume was gentle to my nose. I guess you can say this dark- skinned woman with a low, dark, Caesar haircut was full of style and grace. Her smile penetrated my heart and tears when she smiled and said, "Come with me, Ms. Riley, everything is going to be alright." As we walked down the hallway to the office, she saw the tears streaming down my face. "I'm going to make sure Mark sees you right away," She said.

As we walked into the large -sized office with floor -sized windows, and carpeted floors, Ms. Janice Interrupted him on the phone, saying, "Excuse me, Mark, Riley is here for her appointment." Mark is very polite, down -to -earth, professional, handsome, smart, intelligent, God -fearing, and did I mention cool? Yeah, he's cool. I enjoy talking to him, because he doesn't make me feel like I'm talking to a therapist. Even Though he is indeed my therapist, his words are comforting like an older brother's. He makes me feel like he has my back. He's with the shits," he does not mind calling out dudes bullshit, that I mess with, or even afraid to call out mine during our sessions. This black man is full of enlightenment and wisdom, and he's real. This shoulder-length loc'd hair wearing, cardigan sweater, nicely hugging his biceps, dress pants, with red bottom laced shoes, no creases in them, because he switches up often, He is handsome. I took one look at him and said, now that's a man. He's grown, grown. He doesn't wear much jewelry.

His Diamond Rolex suffices. I was trying to guess his cologne one day, but it's very light and modest. I guess he's truly trying to roll up his sleeves with all of his patient's issues, he has no time to be alluring to anyone's nose, smelling all good. Mark Grey is his name. He tells me the truth, straight, no chaser. Sometimes, I ask for a bit of juice to wash down his realism, figuratively speaking. I've been seeing him for quite some time, so he allows me to call him by his first name. He told me, he allows all his patients to call him by his first name. I guess He wants us to feel comfortable. "Riley, you don't look happy today, what. What happened?" He said with such concern in his voice. I don't want to live anymore. I want this pain to stop. All these thoughts, the torment... He interrupts me, "Riley, what thoughts are you referring to?" Immediately, I began to calm down. I knew that Mark was going to help me get down to the bottom of things. He saw my countenance change, as my shoulders became less tense, and ease came over my facial expression. He offered me a mint as I started to explain to him what was going on. He knows I love peppermints. Mark, I'm not tripping, when I know someone is on my phone. Someone is stalking me. I keep hearing this clicking sound on the phone while I'm talking. "Ok, Riley let's look at this." "Who do you think is on your phone?" It's not the government. I'm not a schizophrenic. This isn't "The Beautiful Mind movie" or nothing like that. The government wouldn't have any reason to be on my phone. I'm not a queen pin, so I know it's not that. It's a loud, weird noise in my phone, like a long beep or something. Something is just off. Please don't say it's me that's off, because I know something is wrong. I looked at him with my eyebrows raised with my head slightly tilted like Arnold from Diff'rent Strokes sitcom. (Mark starts laughing) "No, Riley, I don't think you're off." "Have you been smoking weed again?" No, but I need to burn something, so that I can calm down. This is too much. I might have had some bad weed once, though; that's probably why I'm all messed up now. Mark, do you think the weed did something to my brain, and that's why I'm going through this? "Well, Riley, a lot of times, people spray the weed with different chemicals or lace the weed with other drugs, so anything is possible." No, it can't be anything like that; that sound that I hear is real. I'm not tripping about that. "Riley, why do you think you had bad weed?" "Did something happen to you while you were smoking weed?"

Mark, let me explain. I bumped into an old friend from middle school. We were cool in school, so we exchanged numbers and started talking constantly. This is during the time I was with Dave. Dave didn't mind that we spoke on the phone. Rob was cool and was an old friend. Dave trusted me. Well, anyway, one day, Dave and I were going through it, fussing, and arguing. Rob called me, so I began telling him about our argument. It was basically some petty stuff. I told him I had a couple of dollars, so he said, come through, let's smoke. I thought that was alright, because Dave and I smoked weed all the time. He told me he lived in the Bronx on Decatur Avenue, not far from the Grand Concourse. Now, I know that area is type rough, but I felt I was good and safe, because I was with Rob, and we've been cool since the seventh grade. Even though that was thirteen years ago in the year 1997 and this is now 2010, I still felt like I could trust him. He seems to be the same real one I knew back then. As soon as I got there, Rob greeted me along with this young lady. She was smiling, and she was excited to meet me. Rob and I haven't hung out in years. "Riley, this is Roxy". He said. We both greeted each other with, "Hey girl." and giggled. Roxy looked like what we would call "A hot girl." She had Hair down to the small of her back, she wore fitted distressed jeans, and YSL heels. Quite the beauty too, her Honey brown complexion was flawless, I guess she drank plenty of water. Even the braces on her teeth looked flawless. Roxy was really fascinated with Rob. She said he was the realest dude she's ever been with. She told me Rob was pimping her. (Making her sell her body by having sex with men and women for money). Anyway, we decided to get some Chinese food from up the block from his place. He told me he was renting a room in the area. There's not much green grass and beautiful leaves on the trees on this street. As I walked down the block, I could see people that appeared to be strung out on drugs, nodding from the effects of being high. Young guys walking quickly down the block like they were on a mission, yelling, "A -Yo slime" (Slang language that's often used in the hood to describe another dude or brother). I guess you can call it "the zone," because you can see the drive on their faces to get that work (drugs) off and collect some cash for it. "You want to get a bottle?" "What do you drink?" Rob asked me. No, I'm not drinking tonight. "You sure?" "Come on, let's get a bottle." No, Rob, I'm good. I am hungry, though, with my eyebrows slightly raised showing the intensity of hunger on my face. Why the hell does he keep trying to get me liquor? I thought to myself. I am not interested in getting drunk. He is starting to get on my nerves, asking me about something other than food. "Ok then, since you don't want any liquor, let's walk up the block to the Chinese restaurant." Rob suggested. As we approached the Chinese restaurant, the door was open. Hi, can I get chicken wings, cut up, no tip, with shrimp fried rice, with barbeque sauce and ketchup on the chicken, and a Ginger Ale? I'm not Park Avenue type chic, more like big hoops, long weave down to the small of my back, skinny jeans with some J's (Jordan's) on my feet kind of chic. I'm what you would call a brown skin, high cheekbone, with one dimple honey. I got a little hood to me, just a tad bit anyway. Rob, Roxy, do you want anything? They answered, "Nah we're good." Once I got my food, we began walking toward his place. We passed a few houses and a couple of buildings before we got to him. He lived in a two- family, brick house on a long narrow block, with barely any trees, for a residential area. The neighborhood looks a little run down to have houses on the block. It started getting late in the hour, and dusk was turning into pitch -black night soon. Even the car traffic got fewer. "Come up",," he said, as we stood in front of the porch. "We can sit down, talk and smoke." Rob said. Ok, cool. We walked up the spiral kind of stairs that were near a huge wall. It was so dark in the hallway. I could barely see. I had to feel my way to the stairs. Roxy was rambling about some bread (money) she scammed from this dude she slept with the night before. She was saying something about his Amex (American Express) "Black" Card. I was tuning in and out of what she was saying, as I was trying to penetrate the darkness, squinting my eyes so I could see where I was walking toward. You would've thought I was a tourist, visiting the world-renowned 42nd Street, Times Square, the way I was looking around his house. We walked up the long spiral stairs, his room was on the second floor, on the right side of the hallway near the top of the stairs. The owner must have rented other rooms as well, there. There were a few rooms with closed doors apart from Rob's, with welcome mats in front of them. As soon as we got into the room, Rob could barely flick on the lights before Roxy turned on the Hot 97 radio station. Trey Songz, "Say Aah," was playing, Roxy and I immediately started singing, "And we don't buy no drinks at the bar, we pop champagne cus we got that doe." We were dancing, smiling, and dropping it low (dancing real low to the floor, stripper style). I don't do much dancing, but I can get busy with a two -step or two. Anyway, Rob started rolling up the blunt, which I used my money to purchase. "Aye, shit is lit.," Roxy shouted, waving one arm in the air, while she was singing, smiling, and twisting her small waist, and fat ass around in a slow, wine circle on Rob's lap. He gave her a chuckle and leaned closer to kiss her ass, while holding the blunt with both hands close to his mouth, licking the wrapping paper to seal the blunt closed. I laughed, as Roxy's energy was vibrant and contagious. After the blunt was rolled, the weed cipher started. Puff two and pass, Roxy was cool, we were talking small talk about girly things. Hair, nails, and how niggas be on some shit most times. Rob was laughing and talking shit about how females are trifling too. As the night went on, we kept smoking. I was high as hell, almost to the point of nodding off.

The weed looked a little different than usual, not hard, stiff or sticky, but more like dust material. It was not white, so I know it was not crack, the drug. I'm no expert or weedologist (a person who is an expert about weed and weed smoking), so I didn't think anything of it. Besides, I'm not sure what the drug dust looks like. I mean, is it a dust -looking product? Something like the dust we sweep up after leaving the windows open too long? I'm what you would call "square" to street life at times, not too savvy about what goes on, on the outside, so it's safe to refer to me as Ms. Naive. However, I love the feeling I get from being high and the deep analytical thinking that comes with being high on weed. Other than that, I just don't know too much of anything.

After we smoked, Rob started getting aggressive, Using his strength to push on me a little. "Yo, give me some food, crack that shit open," he said with piercing red eyes. Rob talked, using his hands to gesture. Wait, What? Why are you acting like that, Rob? What's wrong with you? I said in a panic. I couldn't believe his mood switched up quickly. "Bitch, shut the fuck up, and pass that food." Rob, you're talking to me crazy right now. I started feeling scared. I've never known him to get disrespectful with me. I'm getting ready to leave. I said with disappointment in my voice. I looked at Roxy as she was rolling another blunt. "Sis, just relax, he's just playing with you," She said. I could tell he was starting to get angry, so I wasn't paying anything she was saying any mind. I was thinking of a plan of escape."Yo, I'll call you a cab, so sit ya ass back down." "You ain't going anywhere." As I started gathering my things, I said, I'm good. I'll get my own cab. I will flag a cab. I didn't want to wait. I didn't know what was about to happen, but I knew it wasn't anything good. He then snatched my food, took it out of the bag, and started eating it. "Rob chill," Roxy said. She was trying to get him to stop acting like a savage. At that point, he just didn't give a fuck anymore. I was very scared, terrified and high. I stood up with my heart palpitating so fast, as I was reaching for my food; I heard a man's voice say with urgency, "GET UP, LEAVE NOW."

It must have been an angel. I grabbed my things and said I'm out. I was shaking, my heart was still pounding, and my eyes weren't "chinky" anymore. They were wide open, filled with fear. Rob turned into someone I didn't recognize. He stood up and said, "You're not going anywhere," with piercing red eyes. Roxy kept holding his arm and said, "Let her leave, give her back her food Rob." Although his eyes were bloodshot red from smoking, I can still see the seriousness in his eyes. I grabbed my bag and ran toward his room door. He charged after me, but like Forrest Gump, "I was running." The hallway was so dark; I could barely see. I nearly broke my leg jumping down the spiral stairs, trying to get away from them. "You a dumb bitch," he yelled.

"Roxy, get that Bitch." I didn't even look back to see if they were on my trail. I turned the doorknob, barely able to feel for the door. I twisted the knob and yanked the door open. He must have left it unlocked. I jetted out of the brick two -family house and ran in the narrow street, going toward the hill. They call that area the Grand concourse. While I was running, I felt like I was off -balance. I could barely focus. My vision was blurry, my head felt like a ton of bricks, and my legs felt weak and wobbly. It felt like I was just running in place, but I was not; I was moving. However, I had to get away; I knew I was in danger.

Once I got up the hill, there was no car or person in sight. It must have been around 1 am, because the streets were desolate. I was Out of breath from running so fast. My chest felt like it was on fire. I thought, Lord, please get me home safe. The way I was gasping for air, you would've thought I was suffocating. I could barely call on God.

As I looked up the street, I took a minute to regroup and get my breathing under control. I was Barely able to see, bent over, with both hands on my knees, I looked up squinted, Is that a cab? I said out loud, as the bright headlights shined in my direction. That wasn't a cab, I thought. Damn! I whispered under my breath, as my breathing was less labored. I kept looking back over my shoulder to see if they were behind me. Finally, I saw a car, which appeared to be a cab. It looked like a four-door, black, town car. I was so out of it I didn't bother to look down to see if there was "T" on the license plate to verify TLC (Taxi & Limousine Commission) or not. I raised my right arm high, away from my body toward the street, to signal the driver to stop. Once the driver stopped, I took a brief look in the front seat, while running to open the back door. The gentleman looked of Spanish descent, with a mustache. That's all I could remember seeing. I jumped in the backseat. While still nervous, and barely able to see, I said, take me to 174th street and Davidson Avenue. I was scared but relieved. I got away, I thought. I'm safe now. The doors to the vehicle automatically locked once I closed the door. Suddenly, I heard the driver's phone loudly ringing. He answered the phone and said, "I told you to give her some liquor, why? Why didn't you give her some liquor?" I thought to myself, wait, he knows Rob? I thought he was in a cab. OMG (Oh My God), they set me up? He Is not a cab? Is this his friend? He drove really fast down the street. The car was moving so fast. It appeared the streetlights were flashing lights. I just knew we were going to get into an accident. I took a deep gasp of air, holding both hands on the seat, my. My eyes were so wide, my heart was pounding like it was about to jump out of my chest. I said in such a panic, who are you? Where are you taking me? He kept ignoring me, not responding to any of my questions. I looked out the window, as it appeared that we were passing through so many lights, I looked out the window, the lines in the street looked squiggly. This isn't the way to Davidson, I shouted. My shoulders were so tense. My stomach had a knot in it. I thought that was it. So many thoughts ran across my mind, is he going to rape and kill me? Is he going to rob and kill me? I don't have that much money left. Is he driving me to a ditch? What's going on? I grabbed my phone that was poking me in my side. I'm surprised it didn't fall out of my pocket from all the running and jumping I was doing. I scrolled down my Navy blue and silver, Treo cell phone and saw Dave's number. I quickly pressed the button that highlighted his name. Ring, ring, ring. As I was shaking and anxiously holding the phone, I thought, what's taking him so long to answer the phone? "Hello." In a panic, I said, stay on the phone with me, as I was whispering. I spoke so fast and so quietly, he barely heard what I was saying. "What?" "What did you say?" "I can't hear you." Dave said. I didn't want the driver to hear me calling for help, so I whispered again, Stay on the phone with me. While I was looking in the driver's rear view mirror from my back seat, we locked eyes. He saw I was on the phone. "Wassup girl?" Dave said. Please, don't hang up. I thought Dave was still upset with me from our earlier argument. "What's going on?" He said, sounding concerned. Just stay on the phone. I'm in danger. The driver kept saying, "I'm taking you to 174th street and Davidson." He must have heard me on the phone, calling for help. I'm surprised I didn't have a heart attack the way I was overworking my heart with all of the stress and strain. "What happened next, Riley?" Mark, my therapist, interrupted. Dave asked me, "What the hell is going on?" "Why are you whispering?" "Talk to me." He sounded so nervous. I kept telling him, stay on the phone, I'm coming to your house. He stayed on the phone. Once I got in front of the building of Dave's apartment, the driver unlocked the door and said, "Get the fuck out, you silly hoe." I jumped out. I guess he didn't want any money for the ride. I was so paranoid. I just booked it. I heard him yelling, "You stupid, dumb, bitch." I was all kinds of stupid, dumb, bitches and hoes that night, but I was alive, dumb, stupid, bitch, and hoe. It's messed up how, when you need the block to be flooded with people, there are none. Life is strange that way.

When I walked into his apartment, and into the living room, I was still shaken up, but was calming down. Once I calmed down and began to tell him what was going on, he became pissed. He sat on his gray couch with two legs apart, feet planted on the ground, and his right hand on his lap. I sat on the loveseat across from him, with my hands between my legs, with tears in my eyes, while I was hunched over. As I continued to explain the day's terror, I could see the concern in his eyes. He grew very upset. "I knew he was grimey, but you kept saying he was cool." I didn't get a good feeling for him when you told me about him." I told you to stop trusting mothafuckas." "You don't know his ass anymore." "He has changed since the seventh grade." "We're in our twenties now." "If you wanted to smoke, why didn't you come back here and smoke?" "So what, we were arguing." As I was getting undressed, I realized I still had a bag of whatever I thought was weed on me. When I showed it to him, he said, "What the fuck is that?" He smacked it out of my hand and said, "Get that shit outta here." I never saw him so upset. That was a long night. We talked about how shook I was and how dangerous the situation was. He calmed down, and he was glad I was ok. He wasn't the type of guy to go bust (shoot) his gun, I don't even think he owned one, but he was still my protector.

When someone violated me, he felt violated as well, so He began telling me some dos and don'ts when smoking weed with people. "Always watch the blunt get rolled, so you know what's being rolled." He hipped me to the game, so I wouldn't get caught out there again. We settled down, he held me, not saying much, but I felt the security in his arms. Mark sat there in deep thought. Finally saying, "Wow, God protected you." "He saved you from a possible fatality." "Do you still feel like you want to harm yourself?" "Or are you having suicidal thoughts?" I answered, no! I'm ok for now. "Riley, you're not just telling me that because you think I'm going to send you to the hospital, are you?" No, Mark, I'm ok. I mean, I felt ok for the moment, but I was still a train wreck inside, but I didn't want Mark to worry about me. I knew he cared about my well-being, and telling him how I really felt would've caused him to call the ambulance and have me committed to the psychiatric ward. "What are your plans for the rest of the week?" I have work and school. "Ok, I would like to see you again this week." "I know we usually meet once a week; however, I think meeting with me two times a week will be better for now." "Is that ok with you, Riley?" Yes, that's fine. "I trust that you will reach out to me if you start having those thoughts again." "We have to stop here, but please call me if you need me." I grabbed my large Artsy Bag off the couch and said ok, Mark see you next visit. I left there feeling a tad bit better, not quite out the suicidal woods, though. However, talking through what I was experiencing with someone that was non- judgmental and cared for me, helped. I'm grateful for therapy, even though I've been embarrassed to talk about going to therapy with some of my loved ones, in fear that I would be deemed as weak or crazy. It stopped me from quitting life today, but I can't speak for tomorrow.

"The naïve believe anything, but the prudent give thought to their steps." (Proverbs 14:15)

About the Author

S. Rose is a New York-born Writer and Poet. She is developing her craft by working the New York poetry scene and vigorously performing at poetry open mics. Rose has presented her poetry in some of the hottest local stages around the city. She has also presented at the legendary Nuyorican Poets Cafe. Ms Rose makes time throughout the year to bring the art of poetry to various community events. She has even performed her poetry at the world renowned Apollo Theater's legendary amateur night. Ms Rose is also the creator of a poetry workshop series entitled Spoken Thought, which is designed to teach people how poetry can be used as a means of expression, discussion and healing.